# Your Body

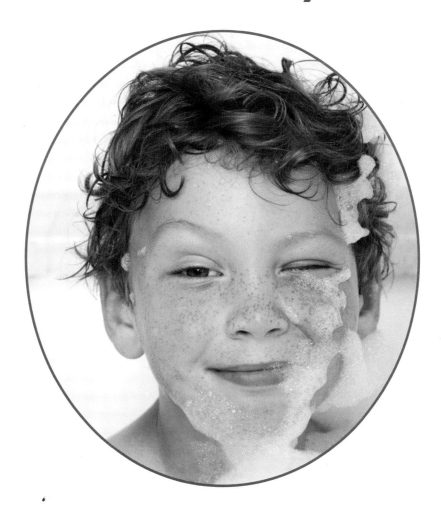

by Margie Burton, Cathy French, and Tammy Jones

Your body is made up
of many parts.

You can see some parts
of your body.

You cannot see some parts
of your body.

Can you name some parts of your body?

The parts of your body help
you in many ways.

You hear with your
ears.

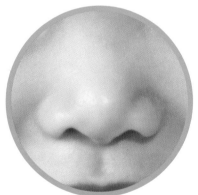

You see with
your eyes.

You smell with
your nose.

You taste with your
tongue.

4

You feel with your hands.

You walk with your legs and feet.

5

There are some parts of your body
that you cannot see.
They are inside your body.

Your heart is inside your body.

Can you feel your heart beating?

Your bones are inside your body, too.

You cannot see them but you can feel them.

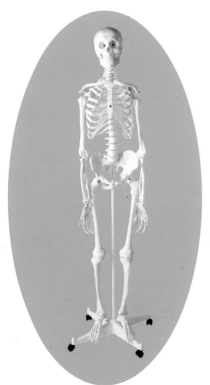

The bones that help to hold up your body are called your skeleton.

8

A doctor can see the bones inside your body with an X-ray.

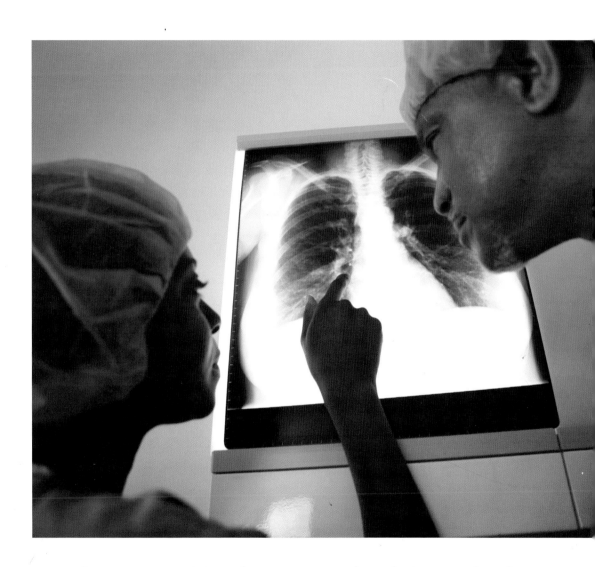

There are 206 bones in the human body.

There are many things you need to
do for your body.

You need to eat.

Some foods are good for you.
Some foods are not.

Do these foods help your body?

Some foods help your body work and grow.

You need to drink, too.

You need to drink water to help your body. Water is good for you.

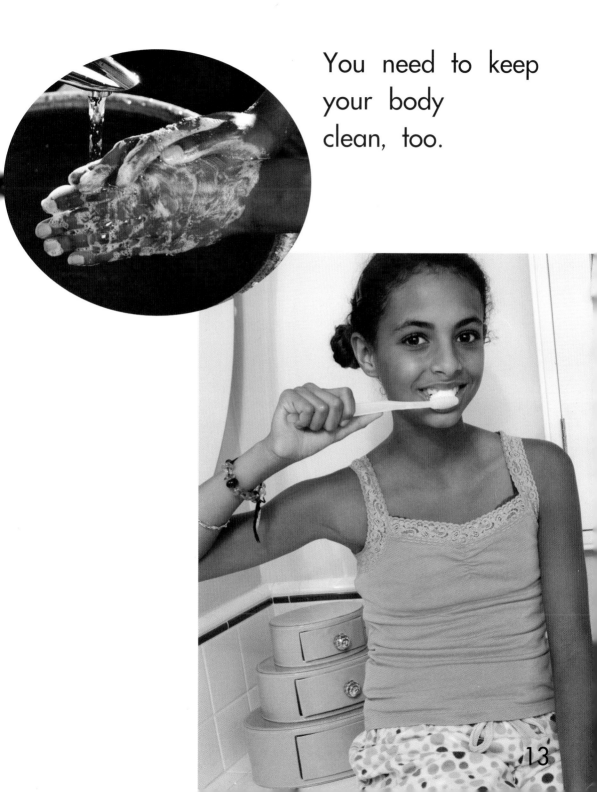

You need to keep your body clean, too.

You need to run and play.
When you run and play,
your body is working.

This makes you feel good.
This helps you to grow.

You need to sleep, too.
This helps you grow.